KU-251-980

WORLD WATCH

THE RED CROSS MOVEMENT

Jane Bingham

an imprint of Hodder Children's Books

WORLD WATCH SERIES

Greenpeace • The Red Cross Movement • UNICEF • United Nations • World Health Organization • WWF

Produced for Hodder Wayland by White-Thomson Publishing Ltd,
2/3 St Andrew's Place, Lewes, East Sussex BN7 1UP

Published in Great Britain in 2003 by Hodder Wayland, an imprint of Hodder Children's Books.

Project editor: Nicola Edwards
Commissioning editor: Steve White-Thomson
Proofreader and indexer: Alison Cooper
Design: Jane Hawkins

British Library Cataloguing in Publication data
Bingham, Jane
The Red Cross Movement. - (World Watch)
1. International Red Cross and Red Crescent Movement - Juvenile literature
I. Title
361.7'7
ISBN 0 7502 4332 5

Printed in Hong Kong by Wing King Tong

Hodder Children's Books, a division of Hodder Headline Limited,
338 Euston Road, London NW1 3BH

Picture acknowledgements: Cover ICRC; title page ICRC; pp4-5 the Federation; pp6-7 ICRC; p8 unknown; pp9-10 ICRC; p11 the Federation; p12 Mary Evans Picture Library; p14 the Federation; p15 BRCS; p16 ICRC (R. Pamu); pp17-18 the Federation; p20 ICRC (T. Mayer); p22 ICRC; p23 ICRC (J Nordmann); pp24-27 the Federation; p28 Imperial War Museum; p29 Imperial War Museum Q2469; pp30-33 BRCS; p34 ICRC (M. Kapetanovic); p35 ICRC (L. Desvignes); p36 ICRC (J-P. Di Silvestro); pp37-38 the Federation; p39 ICRC (P. Spoerri); p40 the Federation; p42 ICRC (T Gassmann); p43 ICRC (U. Meissner); p44 ICRC (J-P. Di Silvestro); p45 the Federation.

CONTENTS

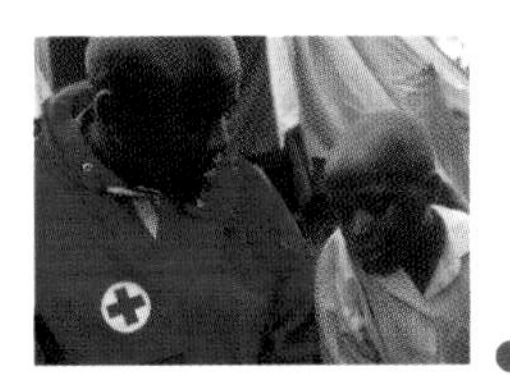

Chapter One: The Red Cross Takes Action

EARTHQUAKE!

In the bustling Indian city of Ahmedabad, people were enjoying a public holiday. A cheerful crowd had gathered to watch a parade of children marching through the streets. Then, suddenly, the ground began to shake, and the nightmare began.

It was like being caught in 'a grinder that kept on turning,' said Mayursidesai, who was at home with his family when the earthquake struck. 'The whole building kept moving backwards and forwards.' Along with his 70-year-old father, his mother and his wife, he just managed to escape by jumping from the balcony.

Others were not so lucky. Survivors, who had fought their way out of shattered buildings, wandered through the streets, dazed and terrified. Parents clawed desperately at the rubble trying to find their lost children. Dead and injured people lay everywhere.

Ahmedabad was just one of many towns and villages destroyed by the quake that hit the state of Gujarat on 26 January, 2001. Altogether, 20,000 people were killed and hundreds of thousands were left homeless.

IMMEDIATE RESPONSE

Within hours of the earthquake, the Indian Red Cross was on the scene. Doctors treated the wounded, while relief workers set up temporary camps, handing out blankets and food to survivors. Tents, food and medical supplies were flown into the area.

Meanwhile, delegates from the International Federation of Red Cross and Red Crescent Societies began arriving from all over the world. Working with their colleagues from the Indian Red Cross, they constructed hundreds of tent cities and set up temporary hospitals.

Within a week, the International Federation had launched a public appeal to raise money for the victims of the disaster. Altogether, 36 million dollars were raised by National Red Cross and Red Crescent Societies in over 40 countries.

◀ A Red Cross worker with local people surveying the damage in Ahmedabad.

A LONG-TERM TASK

Once the immediate emergency had passed, the long-term work of the Red Cross and Red Crescent began. With the help of the International Federation, Indian Red Cross workers began to tackle the job of rebuilding homes, hospitals and schools. The Red Cross is continuing to run disaster preparedness training courses all over western India, so people are better prepared to face any similar catastrophes in the future.

▲ A Red Cross team delivers emergency supplies to a village damaged by the earthquake.

ORGANIZATION IN FOCUS:

Name: The International Red Cross and Red Crescent Movement (often simply known as 'The Movement')

Founded: 1863, Switzerland

Structure: National Red Cross and National Red Crescent Societies in 179 countries, and two international organizations based in Geneva, Switzerland: The International Committee of the Red Cross (ICRC) and The International Federation of Red Cross and Red Crescent Societies (International Federation)

Employees: more than 300,000 employees worldwide; 97 million members and volunteers

Basic tasks:

- ICRC – to protect and help the victims of armed conflict
- International Federation – to bring relief to victims of emergencies and natural disasters
- National Societies – to provide a range of humanitarian services, such as health and social programmes, and to assist victims of disasters and conflicts.

Chapter Two:
The History of the Movement

THE HORROR OF WAR

The idea for the Red Cross Movement was born over 140 years ago on a battlefield in northern Italy. The battle of Solferino was fought in 1859, mainly between French and Austro-Hungarian armies. Both sides had heavy guns, and the battle raged for 16 hours. By the end of the day, thousands of soldiers were left lying on the battlefield – the dead mingled with the living. There was no one to care for the wounded and dying.

However, this terrible tragedy had one positive outcome. A 31-year-old Swiss businessman, Henry Dunant, was on a business trip in Italy when he arrived at the site of the battle. Dunant had no previous experience of war and was horrified by what he saw in Solferino and the surrounding area. 'The approaches to Solferino were literally thick with the dead,' he remembered later. But it was the suffering of the wounded after the battle that affected him most: 'With faces black with the flies that swarmed around their wounds, men gazed about them, wild-eyed and helpless.'

A dramatic 19th-century painting shows a scene from the battle of Solferino. ▼

> "Would it not be possible, in times of peace and quiet, to form relief societies for the purpose of having care given to the wounded in wartime by zealous, devoted and thoroughly qualified volunteers?"
>
> Henry Dunant, *A Memory of Solferino*

Immediately, Dunant set about organizing the people of the nearby town. Young boys brought water, while women washed and dressed the soldiers' wounds. Churches in the surrounding villages were turned into hospitals, and the dead were given a decent burial. Dunant was devastated by the suffering he had seen. But he was also impressed by the willingness of people to help, once someone had shown them what they should do.

DUNANT'S DREAM

Once he was back in Switzerland, Dunant wrote a book about his experiences at Solferino, and outlined his ideas for making suffering in war less horrible. His suggestions included training teams of volunteers in each country so they could help in times of war, providing food and water and medical supplies for the wounded, and letting the families of soldiers know what had happened to them. Dunant stressed that these volunteers should be recognized by everyone as neutral (not involved in the fighting), so that they would be safe from attack. He also emphasized that all the wounded should be given help, no matter which side of the conflict they came from.

Henry Dunant, the Swiss businessman who founded the Red Cross Movement in 1863.

THE MOVEMENT BEGINS

Henry Dunant shared his ideas with four leading Swiss citizens (Gustave Moynier, who was then President of the Geneva Society for Public Welfare, General Guillaume-Henri Dufour, Dr Louis Appia and Dr Théodore Maunoir), and together they agreed to form a working party to investigate Dunant's ideas. In 1863, they set up a 'Committee of Five', which they named the International Committee for Relief to the Wounded. This was the beginning of the International Red Cross and Red Crescent Movement.

Right from the start, the Committee of Five realized that their plans would need to be accepted by many countries. So their first action was to call an international conference to discuss ideas for reducing human suffering.

AN EMBLEM AND A NAME

In 1863, representatives of 16 nations met in Geneva to discuss plans for the treatment of wounded soldiers in war. At this meeting, they also decided that medical staff and volunteers should wear a distinctive emblem in battle so that they could be easily recognized and protected from harm. They chose a red cross on a white background – the reverse of the Swiss flag – to be the symbol of their neutrality. After this emblem was chosen and a number of National Societies had been established, the Movement gradually became known simply as the Red Cross.

A photograph of Red Cross workers and their ambulances, taken in 1876. ▼

This painting shows representatives from different nations meeting to agree the original Geneva Convention. Since the Geneva Convention was signed in 1864, several meetings have been held to add new Conventions.

THE GENEVA CONVENTION

In 1864, representatives of the governments of 12 European nations met in Geneva to sign the world's first international agreement which set some limits on how wars should be fought. This agreement was called the Geneva Convention. It laid down rules for combat, based on the idea of respect for individuals and their dignity. These rules were intended to protect the wounded and sick on the battlefield and to make sure that the people who cared for them were recognised as neutral and were not attacked.

All 12 countries that had signed the Geneva Convention set up Red Cross societies in their own countries. These became known as the National Societies.

FACTFILE: The Nobel Prize

In 1901, the Movement received major international recognition, when its founder, Henry Dunant, was one of two people to be awarded the first Nobel Peace Prize. The Nobel Prize is awarded by a committee of the Norwegian parliament for 'activities of the greatest benefit to humanity' and the Movement has received it four times altogether. In 1917 and 1944, the Movement was recognized for its work in World War I and World War II. It was awarded the Prize for the fourth time in 1963, its centenary year.

▲ Red Cross workers helping the wounded during the Franco-Prussian War. Sadly there were stories of Red Cross armbands being used by thieves to steal belongings from the dead and wounded.

TESTING TIME

The early years of the Red Cross were not easy. It soon became clear that there could be serious problems with the use of the red cross emblem. For example, during the Franco-Prussian War of 1870, many of the French doctors did not wear Red Cross armbands, so they could not be easily identified. Meanwhile, some Prussian doctors were taken prisoner by French soldiers, despite the fact that they were wearing the emblem.

After the Franco-Prussian War, some people said that the Red Cross was a failure. But, in many ways, it had proved itself. National Societies in countries not involved in the war had raised funds for supplies, and sent medical teams to help the wounded on both sides. Red Cross volunteers had worked tirelessly on the battlefield, saving many lives, and assisted disabled soldiers to return to their own countries. During the war, the Red Cross also started a new aspect of its work. Red Cross workers obtained lists of prisoners of war, so they could let families know what had happened to their sons and brothers. The Red Cross also made it possible for prisoners of war to exchange letters with their families.

A SECOND EMBLEM

In 1876, the Red Cross faced a new challenge. War had broken out between the empires of Turkey and Russia. Most of the Turkish soldiers were Muslims, and they associated the emblem of the Movement with the red cross worn by the crusaders in the Middle Ages. The crusaders were an army of Christian warriors who had killed many thousands of Muslims, and many Islamic people still hated the sight of a red cross on a

white background. There were reports of Turkish soldiers killing Red Cross volunteers and then removing their armbands and cutting the red cross to pieces.

In a later statement, the Turkish government announced that they would respect the red cross emblem in battle, but their volunteers would use the red crescent emblem instead. This emblem was the reversal of the Turkish flag's colours, but it was also seen as providing an emblem for those Islamic countries which felt unable to use the red cross because of its association in some people's minds with Christianity. Several other Islamic countries later followed Turkey's example and the red crescent emblem was formally adopted in 1929 when the Geneva Conventions were revised.

▲ A Red Crescent worker from the Islamic country of Pakistan, wearing the red crescent emblem.

FACTFILE: Emblems

Neither the red cross nor the red crescent emblem belongs to the Movement. Both emblems are international symbols of protection during armed conflict, and their use is strictly controlled under the Geneva Conventions. The main users of the emblems are the military medical services. They display one of the emblems – on their buildings, equipment and on the uniforms of their staff – to show that they are neutral and must not be attacked.

THE USA JOINS IN

The Red Cross began as a European movement, but this changed in the 1880s, thanks to a group of energetic campaigners in the USA. These campaigners worked for the formation of an American Red Cross and tried to persuade the United States to sign the Geneva Convention. Among the campaigners was a remarkable woman – Clara Barton.

Clara Barton was working in a government office in Washington during the American Civil War and was shocked by reports of the lack of medical help for soldiers. At great risk to her own life, she visited many battlefields to help the wounded. When the Civil War ended in 1865, Barton set up an office to record where dead soldiers had been buried and to trace the whereabouts of those who had not returned home.

On a visit to Europe in 1869, Barton heard about the Red Cross. She volunteered to help as a nurse in the Franco-Prussian War, and spent nearly four years organizing hospitals. Barton returned to the USA determined to set up a National Red Cross Society there. It took eight years of combined effort from many people, but eventually, in 1881, the American Association of the Red Cross was formed. The following year, the US government signed the Geneva Convention.

A scene from the American Civil War. Clara Barton was horrified that there was no proper care for victims of the war. ▼

A PEACETIME ROLE

By the 1880s, people in the Movement were asking the question: 'Why shouldn't the resources of the Red Cross be used in peacetime as well as in war?' They argued that trained volunteers could do valuable work to help the victims of natural disasters, such as earthquakes or floods.

Gradually, from the late 1880s onward, the National Societies began to play a role in peacetime relief work. However, it was not until the end of World War I that the Movement officially recognized the need for a peacetime role. In 1919 the League of Red Cross Societies was created to co-ordinate the work of the National Societies, especially in peacetime. Meanwhile, the International Committee of the Red Cross (ICRC) continued to organize the work of the Movement in war.

In 1965, the Movement declared its seven Fundamental Principles, which guide all of its work, and in 1991 the League was renamed the International Federation of Red Cross and Red Crescent Societies.

ORGANIZATION IN FOCUS:
The Seven Fundamental Principles of the Movement

- **Humanity** – The Movement aims to prevent and alleviate human suffering wherever it may be found.
- **Impartiality** – The Movement does not discriminate between races, nationalities, religious beliefs, class or political opinions.
- **Neutrality** – The Movement does not take sides in any conflict or dispute.
- **Independence** – National Societies maintain their independence so they can act according to the Principles of the Movement.
- **Voluntary Service** – The Movement is a voluntary relief organization, not prompted in any manner by desire for gain.
- **Unity** – There can only be one Red Cross or Red Crescent Society in each country and this organization must be open to all.
- **Universality** – The Movement is worldwide.

Chapter Three: How the Movement Works

A VAST MOVEMENT

The International Red Cross and Red Crescent Movement is often known simply as 'The Movement'. It is a huge network that employs over 300,000 people across the world. It also has almost 100 million members and volunteers.

TWO INTERNATIONAL ORGANIZATIONS

The Movement has two independent international organizations, both based in Geneva, Switzerland. One of them, the International Committee of the Red Cross – also known as the ICRC – has the job of caring for victims of armed conflict. The other, the International Federation of Red Cross and Red Crescent Societies – known as the International Federation for short – generally operates outside conflict areas. It works with National Societies in four core areas: promotion of the Fundamental Principles and humanitarian values, disaster response, disaster preparedness, and health and care in the community.

THE ICRC

The ICRC provides help and protection for victims of armed conflict, including rebellions and civil wars.

Delegates of the ICRC, who come from countries all over the world, constantly promote the principles of international humanitarian law – this means making sure that all sides in a conflict are aware of the rules of war laid out in the Geneva Conventions and elsewhere.

In war zones all over the world, ICRC workers set up field hospitals and provide relief supplies, such as food, water and tents for civilians escaping from conflict. ICRC delegates also visit prisoners of war, trace the dead and missing and try to restore family links between people separated by war.

After a war is over, ICRC workers provide support for shattered communities, helping displaced civilians to move back into their old homes, rebuilding hospitals and assisting prisoners of war to return home.

A Tracing Programme worker comforts a child who has been separated from his parents.▼

A British Red Cross delegate at work in war-torn Somalia, East Africa.

ICRC Committee and headquarters

The general policy of the ICRC is decided by a committee of 15 to 25 members – all of them Swiss citizens. Their main job is to supervise the activities of the ICRC.

Over 800 permanent staff work in the ICRC headquarters in Geneva. These members of staff co-ordinate the efforts of ICRC delegates around the world, run the Central Tracing Agency and encourage governments to implement international humanitarian law.

ICRC delegates

The ICRC has over 10,000 staff in 69 countries. Many are local people, but some are international delegates. The delegates run the ICRC programmes, which may involve setting up a hospital, visiting prisoners of war, or running a camp for displaced civilians. They may also support the work of the National Society in the country where they are working.

ORGANIZATION IN FOCUS:
The ICRC in 2001

- Average of 800 staff at Geneva headquarters
- Average of 10,057 field staff (1,161 international delegates and 8,896 local staff)
- 69 countries with a permanent ICRC presence, known as a delegation
- 80 countries where relief operations were carried out

THE INTERNATIONAL FEDERATION

The International Federation of Red Cross and Red Crescent Societies was set up in 1919, when it was decided that the Movement had a vital humanitarian role to play in peacetime as well as in war. Its job is to bring relief to the victims of natural disasters, such as earthquakes, as well as emergencies, such as train crashes.

Even after an emergency has passed, the Federation has a continuing role in helping communities prepare better for disasters in the future. It supports health and social care in the community, and also works to promote tolerance and respect for cultural diversity. It is against discrimination of every kind.

Federation Secretariat

Around 200 permanent staff work in the Federation's headquarters in Geneva, known as the Secretariat. Their job is to co-ordinate the work of the Federation's teams and the contributions of different National Societies around the world. They keep in touch with delegates and with the members of the National Societies, finding out what extra help and resources they need, and helping everyone to work together. The work of the Federation's Secretariat is especially vital in an emergency, when they can act very swiftly to pull in resources from all over the world.

Reuniting families – part of the long-term work of the Red Cross Movement. ▼

▲ National volunteers and international delegates working together to give emergency medical help.

Delegates and Emergency Response Units

There are about 340 Federation delegates spread over 63 countries. When a major disaster happens, such as an earthquake, and if the capacity of the authorities and the National Society is overwhelmed, a team of delegates is flown immediately to the area. This group, known as the Emergency Response Unit, is made up of experienced delegates, each with special skills – such as doctors and water engineers. The emergency response team works with the National Society members and delegates in the area to assess what help is needed. They report directly to the Federation's Secretariat, who send in supplies and workers from all over the world if they are needed.

The emergency response team co-ordinates the early stages of a relief operation, staying in the trouble spot until all the teams are in place. Both the International Federation and the ICRC use emergency response teams.

ORGANIZATION IN FOCUS: The International Federation in 2001

- 205 Secretariat staff at Geneva headquarters
- 343 international delegates
- 63 countries with a permanent delegation

NATIONAL SOCIETIES

The Movement has 179 member National Societies and is associated with a further 8 Societies preparing for membership. Most members of National Societies are volunteers, who help people in need within their local community and raise funds for the Movement's work in their own country and elsewhere in the world.

The National Society members play a vital part in the Movement's everyday work, such as healthcare programmes and community care and education. In times of special emergency, such as during war or other disasters, members of the National Societies work alongside delegates from the ICRC and the International Federation.

Community education is a vital part of the work of the National Societies. ▼

Branches and members

Most National Societies have an elected governing council, which makes decisions about how the National Society is run, and a headquarters, with a team of expert staff. The local branches of National Societies have many members – both adults and young people. Each member agrees to give a minimum of 10 hours' service a year, but most give much more.

Emergency response teams

Most National Societies have teams of experts who are ready to respond very fast in an emergency. These teams are used in their own country, but some can also be sent to emergency situations around the world.

National patrons

Many National Societies are supported by famous people in their

country, sometimes working as patrons. National patrons visit members in their local branches, and travel abroad to see delegates in action. These visits provide great encouragement and support for the Movement's members, and also attract welcome publicity and sometimes money for their work.

Working together

Many people inside and outside the Movement have asked how its different parts can function when it does not have a single headquarters. One way that the work of the different parts of the Movement is coordinated is through the International Conference of the Red Cross and the Red Crescent. This is normally held every four years and brings together representatives from the National Societies, the ICRC, the International Federation and the governments of states that have signed the Geneva Conventions. The Conference offers a chance for all these different groups to discuss their plans for working together during the coming years.

ORGANIZATION IN FOCUS: National Societies worldwide

Together, the National Societies have 97 million members and volunteers, and 300,000 employees, helping some 233 million people each year. National Society programmes and services around the world address both immediate and long-term needs and include:

- emergency shelter, food and medicine
- water and sanitation
- restoring family contact for disaster victims
- disaster preparedness
- disaster response
- community-based health and care
- community work against discrimination and in favour of tolerance
- first aid training and activities
- control and prevention of diseases
- HIV/AIDS prevention
- blood donor recruitment, collection and supply.

Money donated to the Red Cross Movement helped to pay for these emergency relief supplies which have been sent by plane to Ethiopia.

RAISING FUNDS

Fundraising for the Red Cross and Red Crescent is a team effort. It involves people at all levels of the Movement, from the staff of the two international organizations in Geneva, who co-ordinate international appeals, to volunteers in local branches all over the world. The work of raising money takes place all year round, but most National Societies and their branches hold a special fundraising week around May 8. This is World Red Cross and Red Crescent Day, the birthday of the Movement's founder, Henry Dunant.

Fundraising in a disaster

When a major disaster strikes, the Secretariat of the International Federation, or the ICRC if it is a war situation, sends out an appeal to all the National Societies. Geneva-based staff also provide the National Societies with detailed information on the scale of the disaster and the funds that are needed, and keep the information up to date.

A National Society might approach individuals and organizations to ask for donations. It might also decide to run a public fundraising campaign, using television, newspapers and the internet. Some National Societies send out leaflets to homes around the country, asking for help. Volunteers collect money in house-to-house collections, and branch members organize a range of fundraising events, from auctions to sponsored walks.

As well as running campaigns for specific emergencies, the National Societies hold fundraising events throughout the year. In many countries, the National Society collects second-hand clothes and other items, either for sale in their shops or to be delivered to less fortunate people elsewhere.

Famous faces

Many famous people have become involved with the Movement, and have helped enormously in raising funds. In 2002, the American Red Cross set up a 'celebrity cabinet' of film stars, rock singers and sports heroes who pledged to support the organization's work. Almost immediately, one of the cabinet members, the film star Jane Seymour, launched a major campaign which aims to fight measles in Africa by vaccinating over 14 million children in Kenya.

Celebrities also hold special events to raise money for the Movement. A rock concert featuring Michael Jackson, Aerosmith, Mariah Carey and Sean Combs was held in Washington, DC on 21 October, 2001. It raised over 17 million US dollars to support the work of the American Red Cross in helping the victims of the September 11 attack on the World Trade Centre in New York.

ORGANIZATION IN FOCUS: International Federation Fundraising 2001

- 35 special appeals for help launched
- 371.7 million Swiss francs (£161.9 million) raised for relief work
- 32.2 million Swiss francs (£14 million) raised for 'capacity building' (support for the National Societies)
- 3.3 million Swiss francs (£1.44 million) raised through special relationships with multinational companies

Chapter Four: **Challenges for the Movement**

WAR AND CONFLICT

Since it was founded, 140 years ago, the International Red Cross and Red Crescent Movement has had to cope with some terrible wars. As well as the two World Wars, there has been almost constant fighting in troubled parts of the world, such as Africa and the Middle East. Many of these wars have been made much worse by other problems such as droughts and floods. In the 1990s, many people in former Yugoslavia experienced the horrors of 'ethnic cleansing'. In Afghanistan, people have been suffering from a deadly combination of war, earthquakes and starvation.

Medical delegates giving emergency help to the wounded in Somalia, East Africa.▼

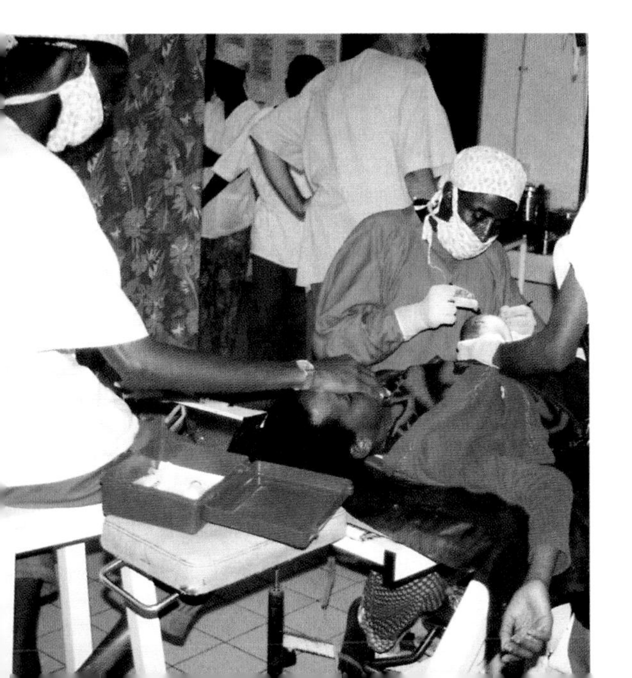

The ICRC in war

For the last 140 years, the ICRC has provided help in conflicts wherever they occur. Wherever there is fighting, it organizes teams of trained doctors and nurses, who are immediately in the thick of it, giving emergency help to the wounded. ICRC workers set up refugee camps for civilians displaced by the war, and its delegates visit military and civilian detainees in prison camps, checking on their conditions and helping them to send messages to their families. Meanwhile, its Geneva staff operate a central tracing system to keep track of the dead, imprisoned and missing.

A unique role

While other aid agencies, such as Médecins sans Frontières (Doctors without Borders) and Oxfam, work just as hard in their work with the sick or wounded and displaced civilians, the ICRC has a unique role in conflict situations. It is recognized in the Geneva Conventions as a neutral humanitarian organization whose task is to protect the civilian and military victims of armed conflicts. ICRC delegates act as guardians of the humanitarian rules of war laid down in the Geneva Conventions. If they see people breaking these rules, they are able to make a confidential approach to the authorities responsible for the incident.

Under certain strict conditions, such as if the humanitarian rules of war are continually broken, the ICRC can speak out against abuses. However, this step is taken only in exceptional circumstances, and only when it is in the interests of the victims. It is not the ICRC's task to investigate offences or to prosecute alleged offenders – this is the task of the governments, either through their national courts or through an international tribunal, such as the International Criminal Court.

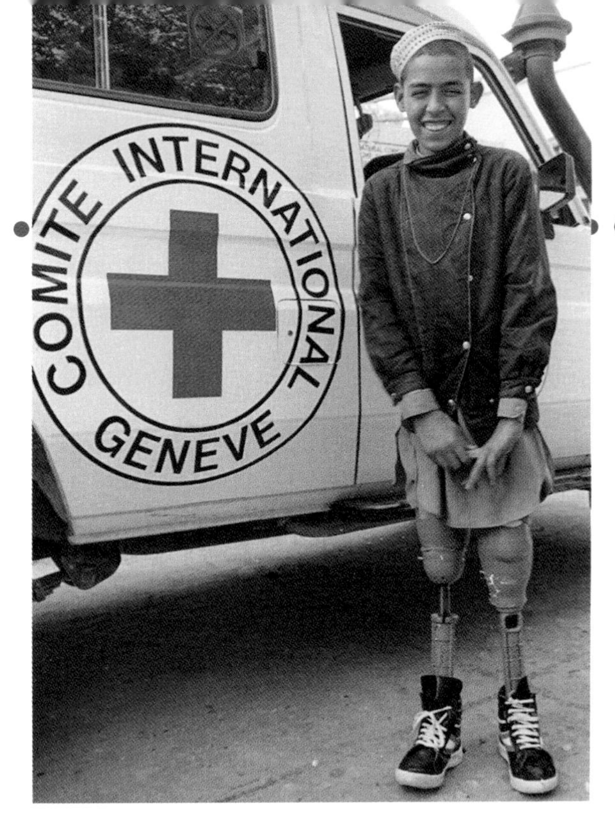

▲ Long-term help for the victims of war: this boy has been given replacement limbs.

ORGANIZATION IN FOCUS:
ICRC war work 2001

- Over 346,000 detainees visited in 72 countries
- Over 865,000 messages exchanged between people affected by conflict and their families
- Nearly 1,900 missing persons traced
- Over 2,700 people helped to rejoin their families
- 1 million people assisted with food, blankets and clothing
- More than 28,000 war-wounded treated in hospitals and first aid posts
- 100 hospitals and 220 health centres supplied with regular assistance
- Nearly 4 million outpatient consultations provided
- Over 9,700 people fitted with artificial limbs.

AFTERCARE

In the early years of the Movement, the ICRC saw its role as restricted to assisting victims during wartime, but people soon realized that the Movement had an important part to play in helping countries to recover, once a war was over. Now, the ICRC withdraws gradually from areas of conflict. Before its delegates leave an area, they try to help rebuild shattered communities and also help to prepare people to avoid conflict in the future.

Rebuilding communities

After a war is over, ICRC delegates work with the International Federation and the local National Society to rebuild homes, schools and hospitals and help people to improve their lives. Engineers set up irrigation systems to water the land and delegates distribute seeds and tools to farmers. The ICRC also sets up special centres, where people injured by explosions can be fitted with artificial limbs.

▲ Delegates and local people working together to build a new hospital.

Changing ways of thinking

As well as providing physical help, the ICRC works hard to change people's attitudes. The ICRC and National Societies run courses on humanitarian law, and the International Federation and National Societies try to spread ideas of tolerance and respect for cultural diversity.

Landmine awareness

One of the most terrible after-effects of modern war is the suffering caused by landmines and other unexploded devices. Long after the armies have left a war zone, innocent civilians suffer dreadful accidents by treading on unexploded mines. In Bosnia, in 1996, 50 people a month were injured or killed by landmines.

> "I was going to the market when I accidentally stepped onto a mine, which exploded and I fell unconscious. When I regained consciousness I was in hospital with acute pain in both my legs... I cried a lot when a paramedic tried to bandage my amputated leg."
>
> Asadullah, a 16-year-old landmine victim in Afghanistan

The ICRC runs courses on landmine awareness. In Bosnia, ICRC staff and the local Red Cross toured schools and villages giving presentations on the dangers of mines. They also helped villagers to set up their own mine-awareness programmes. These efforts have paid off. In 2000, four years after the start of the ICRC public information campaign, the number of landmine accidents in Bosnia had dropped from 50 to only nine a month. Similar programmes are being run in other countries, including a project in Afghanistan run by the ICRC with the National Red Crescent Society.

A Red Cross worker in Cambodia teaching landmine awareness in the local community.

▲ Red Cross workers providing fresh water supplies after a volcanic eruption.

DEALING WITH DISASTERS

The Movement faces enormous challenges from emergencies and natural disasters. It has helped at the scene of earthquakes, floods, fires, volcanoes, cyclones, hurricanes and plane crashes. Disasters like these arrive completely unexpectedly, and need immediate action.

Emergency response

Although the Movement is so large, it can work incredibly efficiently. Within a few hours of a major disaster, like an earthquake, the International Federation sends an emergency response team to the area. This team works with members of the local National Society and delegates to decide on priority needs. It supplies the International Federation Secretariat with a list of needs and within 24 hours National Societies from all over the world can send emergency teams to the area.

Longer-term work

For months and years after a disaster, teams will still be working to put right the damage that has been caused. A year after the earthquake hit Gujarat (see pages 4 and 5), the International Federation and local Red Cross teams were hard at work on a massive rehabilitation programme, which involved the co-ordination of help provided by National Societies from other countries. This included the construction of a 200-bed hospital, 200 village schools and 300 small reservoirs to store precious water.

Disaster preparedness

As well as rebuilding what has been destroyed, the International Federation also works with the local

National Society to prepare people for possible disasters in the future. In India, the Red Cross has set up a countrywide plan, with a national disaster management centre, a national emergency health unit, and stocks of emergency relief equipment stored in eight regional warehouses around the country. A network of community health workers is also being trained to carry out first-aid training in high-risk areas.

> "The earthquake [in Gujarat] highlights how important it is to work to build up our own disaster response capacity as well as the capacity of the local communities. When disasters strike, most lives are saved by affected people themselves before outside help arrives."
>
> Bob McKerrow, Head of the International Federation delegation in South Asia, 2002

PREPAREDNESS WORKS

Following Bangladesh's great cyclone in 1970, which killed half a million people, the International Federation assessed the situation and suggested that the Bangladeshi government should spend money on a disaster preparedness plan and action. The suggestions were accepted, and Bangladesh Red Crescent members built shelters on high ground and organized an early warning system, so people had time to leave their homes before the rivers flooded. In 1991 another severe cyclone struck. Although it took 140,000 lives, many thousands of people survived who would otherwise have died.

A member of an emergency response team assessing the damage after an earthquake.

Chapter Five: Action in Wartime

WORLD WAR I

The ICRC had existed for 50 years when World War I broke out. This was 'total war' as never before. It was fought in many parts of the world and the fighting was continuous. New and deadly weapons were used for the first time – armoured tanks, poison gas, submarines and aircraft with bombs. The war posed the greatest challenge to the Movement so far.

A World War I poster, calling for volunteers to help in the war effort.

At the front

National Societies from all the countries fighting in the war sent medical staff, supplies and ambulances to the front. Red Cross and Red Crescent workers set up field hospitals and worked day and night, and the National Societies of neutral nations, such as Sweden, Norway and Switzerland, also provided help. Sadly, all these efforts could do little to prevent the enormous suffering and loss of life. However, there was one ray of hope – the Red Cross and Red Crescent emblems were generally respected, so medical teams could get on with their work.

Missing persons and prisoners

One of the first actions of the ICRC after the outbreak of war was to set up a tracing agency for missing persons. Over a thousand volunteer workers collected information about casualties and prisoners of war and tried to match it up with thousands of inquiries about missing relatives. This was all done using index cards – a massive feat of organization.

The ICRC was concerned about the way prisoners of war were treated. It sent inspectors to check the conditions in prison camps and organized the sending of over two million food parcels to prisoners. It also set up exchanges for sick and

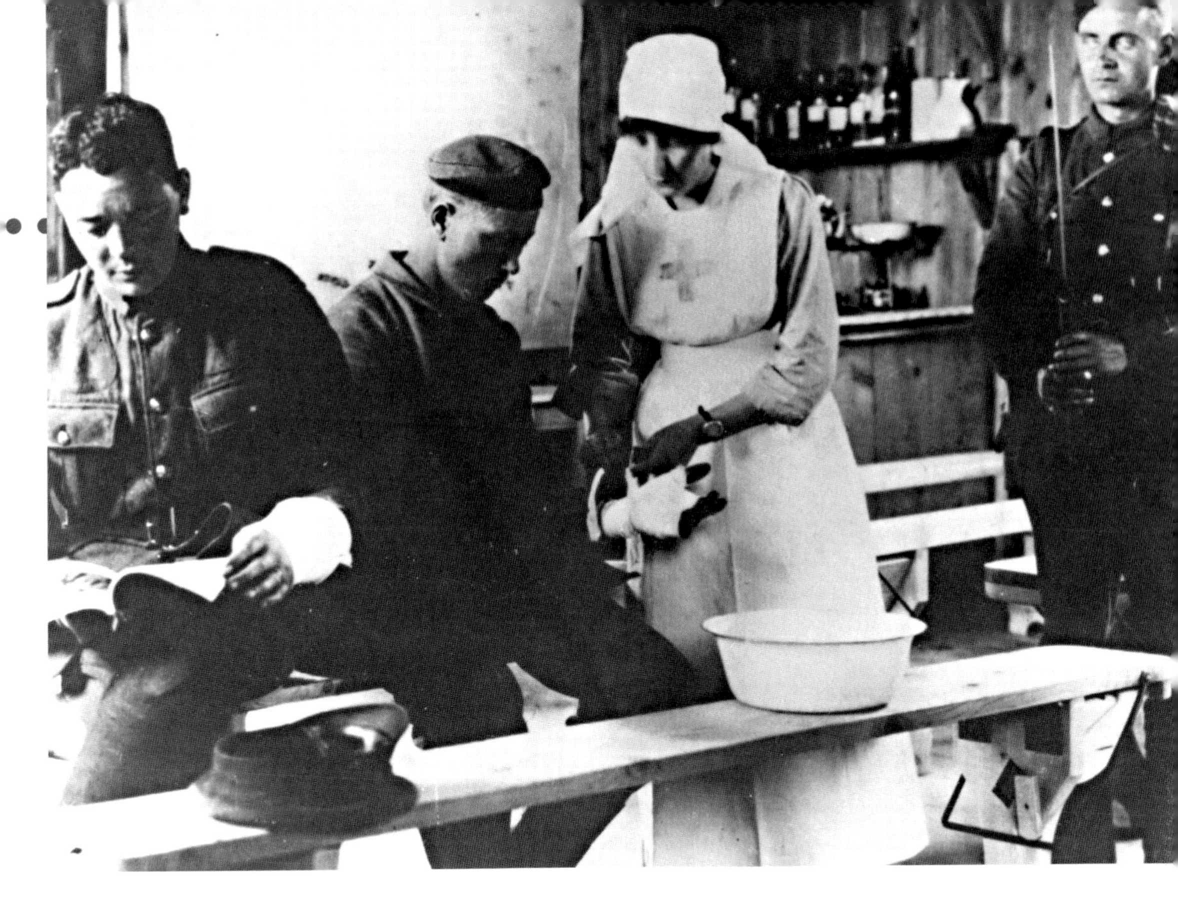

▲ A Red Cross nurse cares for wounded soldiers during World War I.

wounded prisoners, where one prisoner could be 'exchanged' for a prisoner held by the other side, so that both prisoners could return to their own country.

Rules of war

Another task of the ICRC was to check that the rules of war, laid down in the Geneva Convention, were observed by both sides. On land, most countries obeyed the rules, but at sea and in the air, many innocent lives were taken. Clearly-marked hospital ships were sunk and civilians were bombed. The ICRC was powerless to stop these abuses because almost no rules existed for this new kind of war.

As a result of weaknesses in the law seen during World War I, new treaties were adopted. These included the 1929 Geneva Convention Relative to the Treatment of Prisoners of War, and the 1925 Geneva Protocol for the Prohibition of Gases.

FACTFILE: World War I: 1914–1918

- 65 million people fought
- 8.5 million people killed
- 29 million people went missing

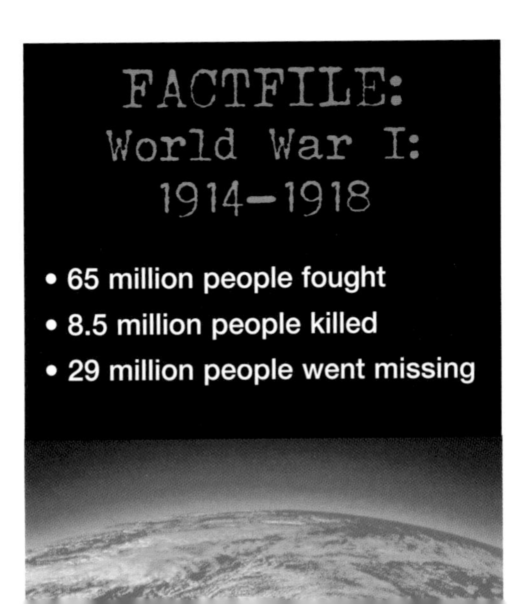

WORLD WAR II

World War II posed many problems for the ICRC. Firstly, it was a war fought on many fronts by armies that kept on moving. This made it very hard for medical teams to provide help for the wounded. Secondly, so many countries were involved that very few neutral nations remained free to give extra medical support. But the Movement rose to the challenge, providing medical teams in areas of conflict, and sending hospital ships and air ambulances to carry the wounded away from danger zones.

Civilian victims

Huge numbers of civilians were killed or wounded in bombing raids in World War II, especially when cities were bombed. This meant that much of the Movement's work was carried out by National Societies inside their own countries. Members worked tirelessly to provide care for the wounded and shelter for people whose homes and livelihoods had been destroyed. Sometimes the work continued long after the bombing, such as in the Japanese cities of Hiroshima and Nagasaki, which were devastated by atomic bombs in 1945.

Looking away?

One of the greatest horrors of World War II took place in the concentration camps, where millions of innocent civilians were put to death. ICRC inspectors checked conditions in prisoner of war camps, but they did

British Red Cross workers during World War II, rescuing civilians from bombed buildings.▼

After World War II, Red Cross volunteers helped to care for the survivors of concentration camps.

not have the legal right to visit civilian camps. The International Committee of the Red Cross was faced with a very difficult choice: should it try to gain access to the civilian camps, but in the process risk losing its right to visit the prisoner of war camps?

Many people think the ICRC should have spoken out more clearly against the concentration camps. They see the ICRC's decision not to take a stand on this important issue as its greatest failure. The ICRC itself arranged for an independent report of its role to be produced, in order to learn from this tragic experience. One lesson learned is that the ICRC should be more willing to make a public statement, as it did on the situations in Rwanda in 1994 and the former Yugoslavia between 1991 and 1995.

After the war

Once the war was over, the Movement played a major role in caring for the victims of the concentration camps. Teams of doctors and nurses were sent to camps like Belsen and stayed for several months, slowly nursing the people back to life.

The ICRC also helped to rehouse the thousands of refugees and released prisoners who were left wandering through Europe after the war. Staff at the Movement's Central Tracing Agency worked for many years, trying to reunite scattered families.

The horrors exposed after the war were one of the main reasons for the decision to include specific provisions about civilians in the revised Geneva Conventions, which were adopted in 1949.

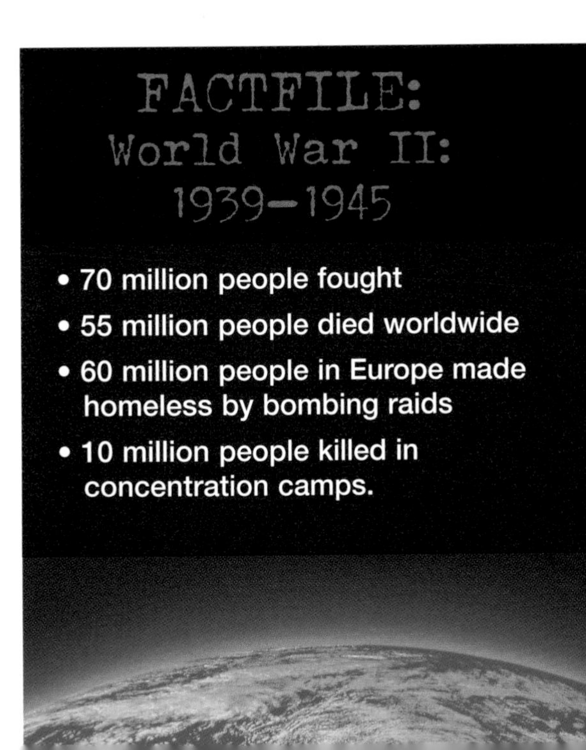

FACTFILE: World War II: 1939–1945

- 70 million people fought
- 55 million people died worldwide
- 60 million people in Europe made homeless by bombing raids
- 10 million people killed in concentration camps.

◀ The terrible situation in Somalia meant that thousands of people were homeless and starving.

NIGHTMARE IN SOMALIA

By the summer of 1992, around 4,000 people were dying every day in the east African country of Somalia. The country was divided by bitter fighting, and most of its farmland had been destroyed. Homeless people fled from gangs of bandits who roamed the countryside, looting homes. The sanitation systems in the towns had broken down, and people were dying from starvation and disease. The government structure had also collapsed, and there was no organization to provide basic care and protection to the population.

Somehow, in the midst of all this chaos, the Somali Red Crescent Society managed to survive. With the help of the ICRC, the International Federation and teams from National Societies around the world, it set up refugee camps on the country's borders and established field hospitals and kitchens throughout the devastated countryside.

Help and support

Working in temporary field hospitals, surgeons operated on the wounded, performing up to 250 operations a week. Doctors treated diseases, and medical staff set up immunization programmes to try to prevent the spread of more disease. Engineers worked round the clock to provide supplies of clean water and rebuild shattered sanitation systems.

Relief workers handed out 'dry rations' such as rice, while other food, such as vegetable oil and beans, was cooked in over 900 field kitchens across the country. The kitchens served mainly women, children and the elderly – those most likely to be robbed when carrying food home.

Trained counsellors provided comfort and support for people who had lost their homes and families, and a message service was set up to try to reunite separated families. Somali farmers were given seeds and tools so they could start to farm their land again. Vets gave vaccinations to sheep, goats, camels and cattle, while engineers set up long-term irrigation projects to water the land.

Dangerous work

Offering relief in Somalia wasn't easy. Aid workers were often attacked and hospitals were raided, even though they were flying the Red Crescent flag. Relief supplies were looted and fights often broke out over how food should be shared. In December 1991, an ICRC worker was shot and died during a dispute over food.

But despite these difficulties, the relief work continued. Ten years later, the Movement was still working to build a better future for Somalia.

"It is difficult to exaggerate the importance of the role played by the ICRC in Somalia. The scale of its assistance, the care with which it has thought out, organized and implemented its programs and the vigour with which it has attempted to bring the plight of the Somali people to the attention of the world have been the nation's lifeline during the last few months."

Independent report by Africa Watch and Physicians for Human Rights, 1992

A field kitchen set up by Red Cross workers in Somalia.

WAR IN BOSNIA

From 1992 to 1995, the country of Bosnia-Herzegovina in south-east Europe was plunged into a bloody war, which killed tens of thousands and created more than a million refugees and displaced people. A quarter of the population was left without permanent homes. Thousands of people, especially Muslims and Croats, were rounded up and murdered in a cruel policy of 'ethnic cleansing', while others 'disappeared' into camps. Towns and villages were blasted to rubble. Water supplies were deliberately cut off and schools, hospitals and churches were shelled.

Providing aid

Working beside other relief organizations, ICRC staff set up camps for displaced civilians. They distributed food, infant care parcels and medical supplies. Doctors and nurses set to work in field hospitals, while engineers began the task of restoring water supplies to villages and towns.

Building for the future

When the war ended, ICRC and International Federation delegates helped to rebuild towns and villages and set up medical and community care centres. They also organized training courses for the army on the laws of armed conflict, and provided counselling for the many adults and children who had suffered terribly in the war.

In September 2000, after years of patient negotiation, a single, unified Red Cross society was created for Bosnia-Herzegovina. This has been a remarkable step because many of the people now working side by side in

Many towns in Bosnia were heavily bombed during the fighting. ▼

the Movement belong to groups that had previously been enemies. Today, the National Society of Bosnia-Herzegovina is working hard with the support of the ICRC, the International Federation and many other National Societies to rebuild its shattered country.

▲ An abandoned tank in a devastated Bosnian village. One of the Movement's biggest problems during the war was finding the people who needed aid. ICRC delegates undertook the dangerous work of travelling to apparently deserted villages, looking for signs of life, and trying to coax people out into the open.

Book of Belongings

One of the greatest horrors of the war in Bosnia was the disappearance of thousands of civilians. This left families in anguish, waiting for news of relatives. In 2000, the ICRC published a 'Book of Belongings', with photographs of clothes, shoes and other possessions found on bodies which were dug up in the city of Srebrenica. Trained counsellors showed this book to people with relatives who had disappeared. This allowed many people to identify dead members of their family, and also helped them to mourn for the dead.

ORGANIZATION IN FOCUS: ICRC aid to Bosnia in 1993

- 160 international delegates and 800 local staff worked in Bosnia
- Relief supplies were distributed to over 1 million people
- The Movement supplied help to 190 medical facilities
- ICRC staff handled over 4 million messages between separated families.

Chapter Six: The Movement in the Community

A WIDE NETWORK

The International Red Cross and Red Crescent Movement has links at every level of society, from powerful international organizations to small, local businesses and community groups. This is what makes it so strong, and its work so effective.

WORKING WITH GOVERNMENTS

The Movement co-operates closely with the governments of all countries, especially those where its members are working. This close working relationship is especially important when there is an emergency and immediate decisions are needed.

Often, the Movement is helped in its work by gifts of money or other assistance from national governments, or from a group of countries, like the European Union. If the Movement needs help to deal with a disaster, the National Societies in each country ask their governments for money and other support.

BUSINESS LINKS

In some countries, National Societies and their local branches develop good

People in Congo, in central Africa, using a water pump paid for by funds donated to the Red Cross Movement. ▼

relationships with companies, individuals and community groups who support them in their work. As well as giving money to the Movement, companies often help to run fundraising events. They also donate valuable equipment – anything from bandages to building materials. Support is also often provided by the media, as television, newspapers and the internet are vital parts of any fundraising or public information campaign.

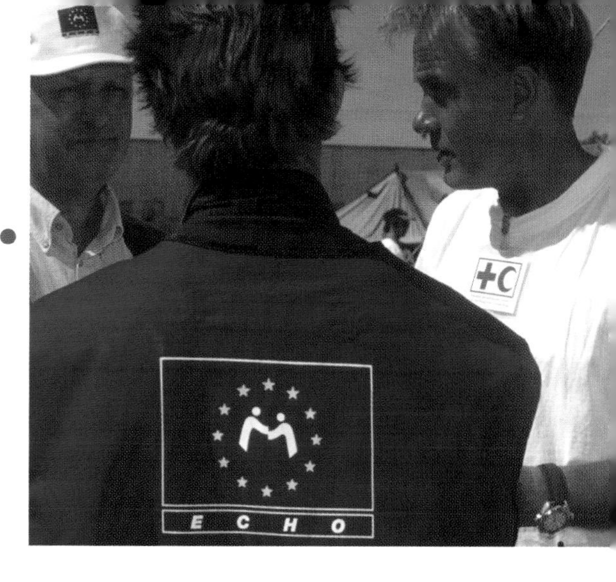

▲ Red Cross delegates often work alongside workers from other organizations.

SHARING THE CARING

The Red Cross and Red Crescent Movement rarely works alone. In Afghanistan in 2002, Red Cross and Red Crescent workers operated alongside many different aid agencies, including Oxfam, Muslim Aid and Christian Aid. They also co-operated with international organizations, such as the UN World Food Programme (WFP) and the World Health Organization (WHO).

This spirit of co-operation between aid agencies extends to all levels of the Movement. The International Federation works with partners such as the UN High Commissioner for Refugees (UNHCR), UNAIDS and the United Nations Children's Fund (UNICEF), to make sure that they all deliver the best possible care. It also works with UN Volunteers, the Inter-Parliamentary Union and other bodies to build a stronger system of volunteering for the future.

FACTFILE: Bears to the rescue

Companies can help the Red Cross and Red Crescent Movement in many different ways. In 2002, the US company Ty Inc., makers of toy bears, created a new white 'America' bear to be sold on the internet to benefit the Red Cross. For every bear bought, the company promised to donate one US dollar to the Movement. Ty Inc. also donates toy animals to disaster relief areas, as playing with toys helps children to deal with the shock.

HELPING OTHERS

Volunteers working for their local Red Cross or Red Crescent branch do valuable work in their own community. In countries like Britain and the USA, being a Red Cross volunteer often involves helping the sick, the handicapped and the elderly. This can mean doing the shopping for someone who finds it hard to get around, or taking a disabled person out for a shopping trip. Red Cross drivers take people to hospital for their appointments. Volunteers often run shops and cafés in hospitals, and some National Societies provide a 'Home from hospital service', helping people to settle back in at home, and visiting them every day to see if they need anything.

National Society youth volunteers are often involved in medical and social programmes such as HIV/AIDS awareness schemes. The International Federation is working alongside other organizations in a worldwide campaign to fight the AIDS epidemic, and also to prevent the discrimination that many people living with AIDS still experience.

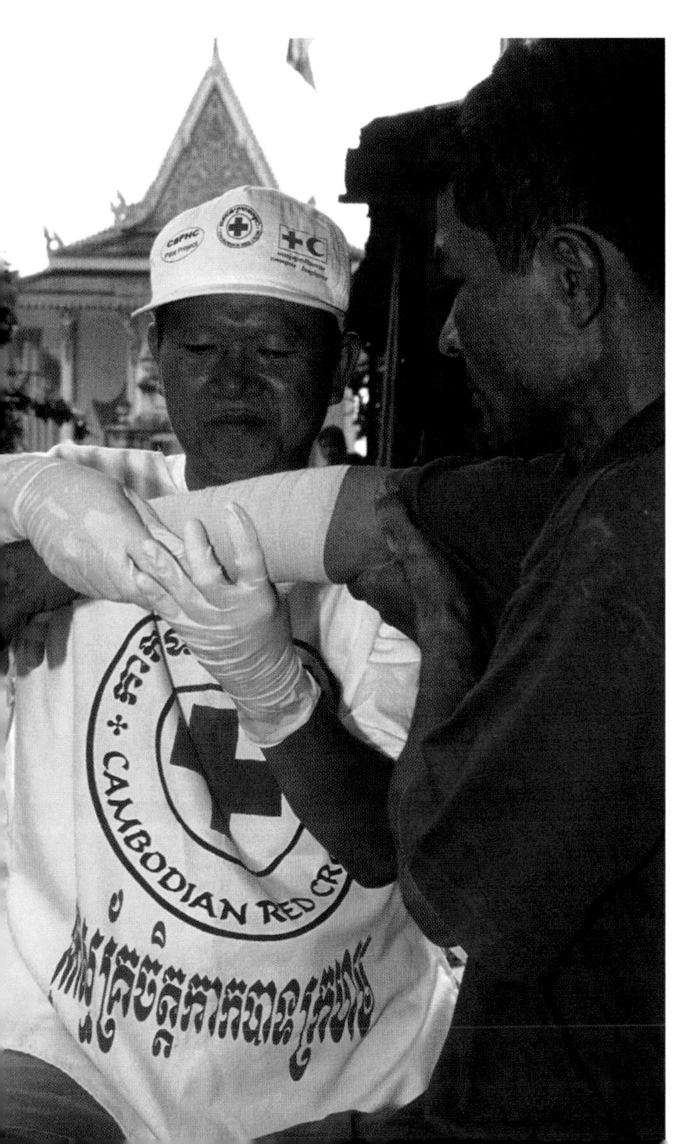

FIRST AID

You've probably seen Red Cross teams and ambulances at local sports matches or fairs. First aid volunteers are on standby, ready to treat and comfort upset, unwell or injured people. They are specially trained to treat minor injuries and carry out emergency first aid. They can also recognize when something is seriously wrong and take people to hospital. The International Federation is running a Global Campaign on First Aid, which takes a range of forms in different countries.

◀ A Red Cross volunteer in Cambodia, giving vital first aid training.

▲ Spreading information throughout a community is a vital part of the Movement's work.

HELP IN EMERGENCIES

Would you know what to do in an emergency? Red Cross and Red Crescent volunteers would. Trained Red Cross and Red Crescent volunteers help ambulance staff, doctors and police at emergencies, such as fires, floods and train crashes. They comfort people who have been involved in the disaster, find them warm blankets, food and drink, and help them to get in touch with their family and friends.

Statistics show that over 95 per cent of the lives that are saved after an earthquake are saved by local emergency services, backed by their own trained volunteers. This is where the Red Cross and Red Crescent really make a difference.

BEING PREPARED

Red Cross and Red Crescent members run courses in first aid – teaching the basic skills that can save lives. In areas where there are special dangers, such as earthquakes or floods, the International Federation and its National Societies run disaster preparedness courses. Training is essential in these cases: members teach people how to recognize the early signs of a disaster, and how to make themselves as safe as possible.

"It was just like the commercials I had seen on television, telling me that the Red Cross is always there when someone needs them. Watching all those volunteers working around the clock in such a tough situation made me really proud to be a part of the Red Cross."

Red Cross volunteer helping in New York, after the attack on the World Trade Centre towers on 11 September, 2001.

YOUNG PEOPLE IN THE MOVEMENT

Since the earliest days of the Movement, young people have been some of its keenest volunteers. After the battle of Solferino, local children helped Henry Dunant by carrying food and water to the battlefield. In later wars, children ran errands for Red Cross teams, and tore up old linen to make bandages. By the time World War I broke out, there were Red Cross youth groups in Canada, Australia, Italy and the USA. Today, youth groups are an important part of National Societies.

Learning about the Movement

Youth groups learn the Fundamental Principles of the Movement (see page 13) and how these ideas are put into practice in the world. Some go on camps, run by adult volunteers, where they practise their first aid and rescue skills and learn more about the Movement. They then become part of the core of volunteers who provide

Youth volunteers can get involved in a range of campaigns. These youth members are planting trees in Thailand. ▼

communities with their strength when disaster strikes.

National Societies know how important it is to keep young people involved, so they arrange international friendship events, linking young people from different countries. These programmes work well: many youth members stay in the Movement all their lives and some go on to train as delegates.

Training for caring

Youth groups learn first aid, childcare and fire prevention. They simulate emergency situations and practise rescue drills. They also help in the community – doing whatever is needed, from visiting refugees to creating safe playgrounds for young children.

ANYONE CAN HELP

Part of the role of youth groups is to let people know about the work of the Movement and raise money for its appeals. But you don't need to be a member to do this. Perhaps you could organize a group in your school to raise money for the Movement, or for a special campaign?

Look in the phone book to find the number of your local Red Cross group. They can supply you with collecting boxes and any other information you need. They may also have ideas of ways you can raise money. There are plenty of fun ways to do it – such as sponsored swims, fun runs or sales.

"Our Red Cross group runs a peer support group where able-bodied kids are partnered with disabled friends. My friend has cerebral palsy. We go to football matches together and sometimes go into town shopping. We have a lot of fun together, and it's also made me realize what life is like for him."

Chris, a Red Cross youth volunteer, aged 15.

Chapter Seven:
The Future

LOOKING AHEAD

As the Movement enters the 21st Century, it faces more challenges than ever before. Many countries are being torn apart by violent wars and rebellions. Worldwide terrorism is now a terrifying force to be reckoned with. Major diseases are sweeping through large areas of the world.

> "[We are facing] a world with increasing tension and recourse to violence, where the need for humanitarian assistance generated by disasters and economic crises is expected to increase: this is a world of opportunity and risk for Red Cross/Red Crescent Societies."
>
> International Federation report, Learning from the 1990s.

The gap between the rich and poor is widening, and our planet is becoming more polluted.

Changes in the world's climate caused by global warming have resulted in more extreme weather – more flooding and more droughts.

CHALLENGES FOR THE MOVEMENT

The Movement also has its own challenges. The number of volunteers is dropping and fund raising is becoming harder. There is now an enormous range of aid agencies competing for the money that people

Food shortages are almost certain to increase in the 21st Century. Here, Red Cross workers prepare vats of food for starving people in the Sudan. ▼

▲ Building health clinics like this one in Sierra Leone, West Africa, is an important part of the Movement's work.

and governments are willing to give. Some people even say they are suffering from 'compassion fatigue' and wondering whether their money can actually make a difference. This is a very negative way to think, because every contribution can help to improve someone's life.

Countries and vulnerable people in need are relying more and more on the Red Cross and Red Crescent to solve their problems. Today, the Movement's job is harder than it has ever been.

A NEW EMBLEM?

In recent years, the red cross and red crescent emblems have sometimes caused difficulties. Although the emblems are neutral and have no religious connections, many people associate the cross with Christianity and the crescent with Islam. This has caused problems, especially in some civil wars where one side has been identified with Christians and the other with Muslims. In addition, the Israeli National Society uses the red shield of David as its emblem, and because of this is currently unable to become a full member of the Movement.

What is the solution?

The Movement is asking governments (who are the legal owners of the Geneva Conventions and the primary users of the red cross and red crescent emblems) to create another protective emblem which would be seen as genuinely neutral by all sides in a war. It could also be used by National Societies who feel unable to use either the cross or the crescent. This new emblem will not replace the red cross or the red crescent in the countries where these are used.

A major issue facing the Movement in the 21st Century is the involvement of children in war.

UNIFYING THE MOVEMENT

People have often questioned how the Movement can operate efficiently when it has two international organizations at its head – the ICRC and the International Federation, as well as over 170 National Societies.

From the early 1990s onwards, it became increasingly obvious that a clear plan was needed for how all the parts of the Movement could improve their work together. The first major step towards this aim was taken in 1997 at a conference in Seville, when the ICRC, the International Federation and the National Societies agreed to co-operate more closely, both in planning and in response to emergencies. In particular, it was decided that they should define which was the 'lead agency' in any emergency situation so that the members of the Movement would know which organization was co-ordinating the total response.

Two years later, in 1999, a working group, made up of representatives from the ICRC, the International Federation and the National Societies was set up to create a long-term plan for the whole Movement. It published its findings in 2001 in a document called *Strategy for the Movement*.

STRATEGY FOR THE MOVEMENT

The *Strategy* sets out three main aims. Firstly, it aims to strengthen each of the components of the Movement, concentrating especially on the National Societies. It plans to provide systematic training for National Society leaders, using a network of experts drawn from both the ICRC and the International Federation. It also plans to create a shared set of guidelines and targets to be followed by National Societies throughout the world, and believes that these measures will lead to improved recruitment of local volunteers.

The second aim of the *Strategy for the Movement* is to increase the Movement's efficiency by better communication and co-operation between its components, especially in emergency situations.

Thirdly, the *Strategy* aims to improve the Movement's image and its relations with governments and external partners, such as international organizations and large companies in the private sector.

PLANNING FOR THE FUTURE

Throughout the Movement, people are looking ahead and working out new ways to meet the challenges of the 21st Century. All the Movement's plans for the future rely on the hard work of its members and supporters. Whether they are working in one of the world's trouble spots, helping in their local community, or raising funds, it is the members who make the Movement work. And in the future, you could be one of those members.

"I dream of a Red Cross and Red Crescent Movement capable of engaging the vital forces of all nations and especially the youth, eager to commit themselves to a cause which transcends nations."

From the *Strategy for the Movement* document.

Red Cross and Red Crescent delegates working together. In the future, the Movement will need to be even more unified to tackle the world's problems. ▼

abuse To use something wrongly, or to break some rules.

atomic bomb A very powerful bomb that can destroy an entire city. Atomic bombs also have long-term health effects, causing cancer.

blood donor Someone who gives some of their blood to be stored and later given to somebody else.

campaign A series of actions organized over a period of time in order to achieve something. Red Cross and Red Crescent campaigns often involve raising money as well as raising public awareness of humanitarian issues.

Central Tracing Agency A special organization set up by the ICRC to record and help find out what has happened to people who have been killed, lost or imprisoned during a conflict.

civilian Someone who is not a member of the armed forces.

concentration camp During the Second World War Hitler's Nazi party sent Jews, 'gypsies' and other groups of people to special camps. People lived in terrible conditions in these concentration camps and many were killed there.

confidential Private or secret.

counsellor Someone who is trained to listen to people's problems and provide support and understanding.

cyclone A very strong storm in which the wind blows in a spiral.

delegate A staff member of the Red Cross and Red Crescent Movement who works as part of a team in a foreign country.

detainees People who are kept as prisoners without trial and not allowed to go free.

development Work done over time to help improve a situation.

displaced Forced to leave your home because of a war or disaster, but still inside your own country.

drought A long spell of very dry weather that causes harvests to fail.

emergency response unit A team that reaches a disaster site very fast and decides what help is needed.

ethnic cleansing An attack on people of a particular race or religion, often involving driving them from their homes or killing them.

famine A serious shortage of food.

field hospital A temporary hospital set up in a trouble spot.

fronts Areas where battles are fought.

Fundamental Principles The most important beliefs and guiding ideas of the Movement (see page 13).

Geneva Conventions A set of rules for countries fighting wars (see page 9).

humanitarian Helping people in need simply because they are fellow human beings.

immunization programme A plan to give people injections to protect them from diseases.

irrigation system A method of bringing water to land, so that the land can be used for farming.

landmine A small bomb that lies close to the surface of the ground, and explodes when someone treads on it.

medical facility A hospital or a health centre.

National Society A country's Red Cross or Red Crescent Society.

neutral Not taking sides in a war or other conflict.

patron Someone who supports a group, by giving time or money to it.

policy A set of rules or ideas which guides action.

priority Something that is more important than other things.

refugee Someone who has been forced to leave his or her home and enter another country because of a war or a disaster.

rehabilitation programme Activities to help people to begin a normal life again.

sanitation A system of sewers and drains to carry away waste.

secretariat The staff who work at an organization's head office.

simulate To pretend.

standby Ready to be used if needed.

tribunal A court or a meeting in which legal decisions are made.

UN United Nations. The UN is an international organization, representing countries from all over the world, which tries to solve world problems.

vaccination An injection that protects a person or an animal from getting a disease.

volunteer Someone who works without receiving any payment.

FURTHER READING

Books for younger readers

British Red Cross, New Practical First Aid, British Red Cross (Dorling Kindersley, 1999)

Clara Barton, Wil Mara (Children's Press, 2002)

International Red Cross, Ralf Perkins (Franklin Watts, 2000)

British Red Cross, Louise Spilsbury (Heinemann, 2000)

The Red Cross Story, Emily Wood (Dorling Kindersley, 1995)

Books for older readers

Dunant's Dream, Caroline Moorhead (Harper Collins, 1998)

USEFUL ADDRESSES

International Committee of the Red Cross
19 Avenue de la Paix, CH-1202 Geneva
Switzerland
www.icrc.org

International Federation of Red Cross and Red Crescent Societies
P O Box 372, CH-1211 Geneva 19
Switzerland
www.ifrc.org

The British Red Cross
9 Grosvenor Crescent
London SW1X 7EJ
www.redcross.org.uk

The American Red Cross
431 18th Street, NW
Washington, DC 20006, USA
www.redcross.org

The Australian Red Cross
P O Box 196
Carlton Vic 3053
Australia
www.redcross.org.au

INDEX